Down on the Farm

CHICKENS

Hannah Ray

QED Publishing

QED

First published in the UK in 2006 by
QED Publishing
A Quarto Group company
226 City Road
London EC1V 2TT
www.qed-publishing.co.uk

A Catalogue record for this book is available
from the British Library.

ISBN 1 84538 467 9

Written by Hannah Ray
Designed by Liz Wiffen
Consultant Sally Morgan
Editor Paul Manning
Picture Researcher Joanne Forrest Smith
Illustrations by Chris Davidson

Publisher Steve Evans
Editorial Director Jean Coppendale
Art Director Zeta Davies

Printed and bound in China

CONTENTS

Words in **bold** can be found in the Glossary on page 22.

Chickens on the farm

Do you know where we get eggs for breakfast, and the tender white meat that tastes so good in salads, sandwiches and barbecues?

Both of these types of foods come from chickens.

Farmers all over the world keep chickens. In fact, there are more chickens in the world than people!

Chickens from beak to tail

A fully grown chicken is about 40cm tall and weighs around 3kg – the same as three bags of flour.

Eyes

Wings

Beak
(chickens
do not have
any teeth)

Feet

Comb

Wattle

Height of
six-year-old child

FARM FACT
Chickens have wings
but they can only fly
short distances. The
longest recorded flight
by a chicken is
13 seconds.

Height of
chicken

Male chickens, called
cockerels or roosters,
have a **wattle** and
a **comb**. Cockerels
have more colourful
plumage than
female chickens.

7

It's a chicken's life...

A **chick** starts life as an egg inside its mother. After the egg has been laid, the mother chicken, or hen, sits on it to keep it warm and turns it over and over.

After 21 days, the chick uses a special egg tooth on its beak to chip its way out of the egg.

8

FARM FACT
A hen clucks to her chick while it is still inside the egg.

Newborn chicks have soft, fluffy feathers. After eight days, other feathers start to grow.

After two months, the chick has most of its grown-up feathers. By four and a half months, it is fully grown. A female chicken is now old enough to lay her own eggs.

Most chickens live for about seven years.

9

Who rules the roost?

In a henhouse, some hens are more important than others. This special order of importance is called a pecking order, because the hens peck and bully one another to find out who is boss!

Bigger, stronger hens take the highest **perches** in the henhouse. The chickens that are lower down the pecking order stay away from the bigger chickens and hold their heads low.

11

Egg-citing!

Different types of chickens
lay different-coloured eggs.
Most hens lay eggs with
white or brown shells,
but some hens' eggs
are pink, blue or
even green!

An egg yolk

The colour of
the **yolk** depends
on what the hen has been
eating. Hens that eat lots of
grass and vegetables lay eggs
with rich orange-yellow yolks.

12

Free-range eggs come from chickens that are free to wander outside.

FARM FACT
A hen will lay a new egg about every one to one and a half days. Most hens lay about 250 eggs a year, but some lay as many as 320.

You can tell if an egg is fresh by placing it in a bowl of water. If the egg is fresh, it will sink. If the egg is old, it will float.

13

Eggs, meat and feathers

Farmers keep
chickens for their
meat as well as their
eggs. Chickens that give us eggs
are called layers. Chickens kept for
meat are called broilers or table birds.

14

Scientists have
found out that
parts of a chicken's
feathers are very
absorbent. This
means they are good
at soaking up liquid.

Feathered friends

PRAIRIE CHICKEN

These chickens come from North America. The males have a special orange patch on their necks which they puff up to attract female chickens.

POLISH BANTAM

Famous for their amazing feathers, these small chickens come from Poland. Some of them even have beards, too!

FARM FACT
Chickens make great alarm clocks! Farmers today still wake up to the sound of cockerels crowing.

FRIZZLE

Frizzle chickens are easy to spot. Their feathers curl back towards their heads, rather than lying flat and pointing towards their tails.

RED JUNGLE FOWL

This chicken lives in Asia and eats seeds, fruit and insects. The Red Jungle Fowl is the chicken that all other chickens came from.

Chickens around the world

UKRAINE

Decorating hens' eggs for Easter is a **tradition** in many countries. An Easter egg from the Ukraine is called a 'pysanka'. The beautiful pictures and patterns on these eggs mean different things, from happiness to good luck.

CHINA

In China, each year is named after one of twelve animals. People born in the Chinese Year of the Rooster are hard-working and brave.

18

Egg-racing with hand-painted eggs on the White House lawn.

AMERICA

Every year an 'Easter Egg Roll' takes place on the lawns of the White House in Washington DC, the home of the American president. The Easter Egg Roll started in 1878 and is still going today.

19

Make your own chirpy chicks

Have fun making a box of chirpy chicks!
All you need is a box of six eggs, a pin,
a bowl and some paints.

1 Ask a grown-
up to use a pin to
make a hole at the
top and bottom of
an egg.

2 Hold the egg over
a bowl and blow into
the hole at the top.
If you blow hard, the
yolk and white will
come out of the hole
at the bottom.

3 Hold the egg under the tap and run water through it to clean it out.

BRIGHT IDEA
Ask a grown-up to help you use the leftover egg whites and yolks to make a cake.

4 Paint your blown egg to look like a little chick.

5 Blow the other eggs and paint them until you have a set of chirpy chicks! Try adding googly eyes or fluffy feathers (you can buy these from a craft shop) and stick them on with glue.

Glossary and Index

chick   baby chicken

comb   a flap of skin on the top of a cockerel's head

perch   where a chicken sits, rests and sleeps

plumage   feathers on a chicken

tradition   something that is passed on from parents to their children, and then on to their children

wattle   flap of skin hanging from the neck of a bird

yolk   yellow part in the middle of a hen's egg

Ideas for teachers and parents

- Research pictures of different breeds of chickens and use them to make a poster. You could make factsheets comparing the children's favourite breeds.

- Look at pictures of hens and cockerels of the same breed. How do they differ?

- Take a clean yoghurt pot. Thread a needle with cotton and carefully push it through the base of the pot. Tie a knot in the end of the cotton. Tug on the cotton to make a clucking sound. Running your fingernail down the cotton will produce a longer cluck!

- Make a chicken collage. Draw the outline of a chicken on a large piece of paper. Look through magazines, newspapers, supermarket fliers, etc., and cut out anything related to chickens, chicks and eggs. Collect feathers, scraps of material and other bits and pieces. Stick down everything you have collected to fill in the chicken outline.

- Draw a chicken outline on a piece of A4 paper. Photocopy it a few times and challenge the children to design some funky feathered plumage. Encourage them to be bold and wacky and to use bright colours. They could add impressive combs and experiment with different shapes for the feathers.

- Make a wordsearch for the children using chicken-related vocabulary from this book.

- If possible, visit a children's farm so the children can see real chickens.

- See how many jokes, stories, poems and rhymes about chickens the children can think of. Can they make up a chicken poem of their own?